The Life of a
FROG

Ple
Ple

Re

Textp
speec

www.her

Clare Hibbert

www.raintreepublishers.co.uk
Visit our website to find out more information about **Raintree** books.

To order:
☎ Phone 44 (0) 1865 888112
▤ Send a fax to 44 (0) 1865 314091
▢ Visit the Raintree Bookshop at **www.raintreepublishers.co.uk** to browse our
catalogue and order online.

First published in Great Britain by Raintree,
Halley Court, Jordan Hill, Oxford OX2 8EJ,
part of Harcourt Education.
Raintree is a registered trademark of Harcourt
Education Ltd.

Editorial: Nick Hunter and Catherine Clarke
Design: Michelle Lisseter and Tipani Design
    (www.tipani.co.uk)
Illustration: Tony Jones, Art Construction
Picture Research: Maria Joannou and Ginny
    Stroud-Lewis
Production: Jonathan Smith

Originated by Dot Gradations Ltd
Printed and bound in China by South China
Printing Company

ISBN 1 844 43317 X (hardback)
08 07 06 05 04
10 9 8 7 6 5 4 3 2 1

ISBN 1 844 43324 2 (paperback)
09 08 07 06 05
10 9 8 7 6 5 4 3 2 1

British Library Cataloguing in Publication Data
Hibbert, Clare
The Life of a Frog. – (Life Cycles)
571.8'1789
A full catalogue record for this book is available
from the British Library.

Acknowledgements
The publishers would like to thank the following
for permission to reproduce photographs:
A-Z Botanical p.**4**; Alamy Images p. **18**; DK Images
p.**27**; FLPA (Roger Tidman) pp.**20**, **28**; Getty
Images p.**29**; Holt Studios p.**12**; Nature Picture
Library (Fabio Liverani) p.**23**; NHPA pp.**9** (Eric
Soder), **11** (Stephen Dalton), **13** (Stephen Dalton),
14 (Stephen Dalton), **16** (G. I. Bernard); Oxford
Scientific Films pp.**5** (Maurice Tibbles), **10**
(Paul Franklin), **15** (Michael Leach), **17** (London
Scientific Films), **19** (London Scientific Films),
21, **22**, **24**, **25**; Premaphotos Wildlife p.**8**;
Science Photo Library (Gary Meszaros) p. **26**.

Cover photograph of a common frog, reproduced
with permission of Corbis (George McCarthy).

The publishers would like to thank Janet Stott for
her assistance in the preparation of this book.

Every effort has been made to contact copyright
holders of any material reproduced in this book.
Any omissions will be rectified in subsequent
printings if notice is given to the publishers.

The paper used to print this book comes from
sustainable resources.

Contents

Any words appearing in bold, **like this**, are explained in the Glossary.

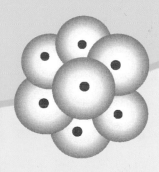

The frog

Frogs belong to a family of slimy-skinned animals called **amphibians**. Like all amphibians, frogs live a double life. They spend part of their lives in water and part on land. **Adapting** to these different homes, or **habitats**, involves big life changes.

Frogs can swim in water or leap on land.

4

Growing up

Just as you grow bigger year by year, a frog grows and changes, too. As a baby, or tadpole, it can survive only in water. As it grows, its body changes to cope with life on land.

There are thousands of different types of frog but they all go through the same basic changes. The different stages of the frog's life make up its **life cycle**.

Where frogs live

Adult frogs live all over the world, except in places that are very cold. They stay near to ponds and streams, where they can lay their eggs.

Young frogs, called tadpoles, look nothing like their parents.

A frog's life

The frog's **life cycle** starts in spring. Female frogs lay masses of jelly-like eggs in streams and ponds. Ten days later a tiny, dark tadpole wriggles out of each egg.

Big changes

At first, a tadpole looks more like a fish than a frog. It has **gills** and a tail. Over the next three months it gradually sprouts four frog's legs and loses its fishy tail. Slowly, the tadpole turns into an adult frog.

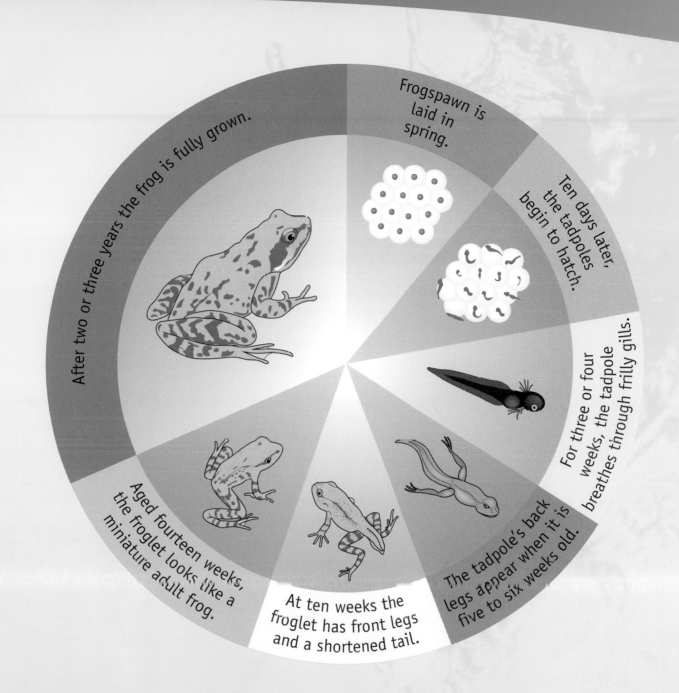

Frogspawn is laid in spring.

Ten days later, the tadpoles begin to hatch.

For three or four weeks, the tadpole breathes through frilly gills.

The tadpole's back legs appear when it is five to six weeks old.

At ten weeks the froglet has front legs and a shortened tail.

Aged fourteen weeks, the froglet looks like a miniature adult frog.

After two or three years the frog is fully grown.

This diagram shows the life cycle of a frog, from egg to adult.

Mating time

In spring, adult frogs visit ponds to lay their eggs. Any fresh water will do – streams, boggy ditches or even rain-filled tractor tracks! Slow-moving water that will not churn up the eggs is best.

Have you ever heard a chorus of frogs croaking? That is the sound of male frogs trying to attract females. When a female comes close, the male hugs her from behind. He has pads of rough skin on his fingers that help him hold on to her slippery body.

When he is about to sing, the male frog puffs out his throat.

Eggs away!

As the female lays her eggs in the water, the male covers them with his **sperm** to **fertilize** them. **Mating** can last for several days. When the female has no more eggs to lay, the two frogs separate. They do not stay to look after the eggs.

How many eggs?

Many female frogs lay around 100 eggs – but some types can lay thousands! Only a few of these eggs will survive to be adult frogs.

Frogs lay their eggs in spring, when the water is not too cold and not too warm.

Frogspawn features

Each egg – a black dot – is safe inside a pea-sized ball of jelly. The balls stick together to form a clump called **frogspawn**. The jelly cushions the eggs. It makes them too slippery for water creatures to eat, or for mould to grow on. It also keeps the eggs warmer than the water around them.

Each egg is safe inside a ball of jelly. At first the eggs are perfectly round.

Egg action

Not all of the eggs will **hatch.** Some die because conditions are not quite right. These eggs go a milky colour. In the healthy eggs, the black dot begins to change shape. After about four days, the black dot has become bean-shaped. After one week, it begins to look like a tadpole, with a head and tail. **Yolk** inside the egg feeds the tiny, growing tadpole.

In these week-old eggs, tiny tadpoles are taking shape.

Spawning toads

Toads are close relatives of frogs. They lay their eggs in ponds, too, but their eggs do not clump together like frogspawn. The eggs form long chains that wrap around pond plant stems.

Wriggling out

After about ten days, the jelly around the tadpole softens. The tadpole can wriggle around inside it. Now it is ready to **hatch**. The tadpole is tiny and very weak. It stays near to the other eggs and baby tadpoles.

At first, the tadpole cannot open its mouth, but it does not go hungry. Its meals for its first day or two are already in its **abdomen** – the lower part of its body. The abdomen is full of **yolk** from the egg.

A tadpole slips out of its jelly ball and into the water of the stream or pond.

Sticky business

The patch of skin between the tadpole's mouth and belly is sticky. This lets the tadpole stick itself to a piece of pondweed so it will not be swept away by fast-flowing water. The tadpole rests here until its mouth opens. By the time this happens, the tadpole is strong enough to swim off in search of food.

The baby tadpoles stay close together as they search for food.

The tadpole spends a lot of time near the surface, or at the shallow edges, of the pond. Here the water is warmer, because it has been heated by the sun. The tadpole does not need to be near the surface to breathe – it can breathe under water, just like a fish.

The tadpoles nibble on pond plants.

Pond plants

All sorts of plants grow in the pond. Dots of bright green duckweed float on the surface. Fuzzy shoots of pondweed rise out of the mud. As well as making oxygen, plants feed many of the creatures in the pond, including the young tadpoles.

Breathing liquid

The tadpole has frilly **gills** on the outside of its body. They look like feathers on either side of its head. They take in **oxygen** from the water. Oxygen is the gas that animals need to breathe. Plants put fresh oxygen into the water.

 gills

Gills on each side of the tadpole's head allow it to breathe under water.

No frills

By the time the tadpole is four weeks old, its frilly, outside **gills** have disappeared. They have been covered with skin. The tadpole can still breathe under water, however, through gills that are inside its body. These gills are even more like a fish's gills, because they are protected by a flap of skin.

By four weeks old, the tadpole has gills inside its body.

Teething tadpole

Around this time, the tadpole grows tiny teeth. With these it can gnaw and nibble on larger pieces of pondweed. It now stays near the bottom of the pond, feeding and building up its strength. At first, tadpoles are plant-eaters, or **herbivores**. Later, the tadpole will start to include some meat in its diet.

A meat-free diet

Plants do not contain as much energy as meat, so the tadpole eats almost all the time. Plants are also difficult to **digest**. The tadpole's **abdomen** is large compared to the rest of its body. The long gut gives the tadpole time to break down the plants and take in the **nutrients**.

At this stage of its life, the tadpole eats almost all the time.

Finding its feet

At around five weeks, the tadpole's back legs start to grow. Each ends in a tiny, webbed foot with five budding toes. In a few months, these feet will act as flippers to push the adult frog through the water. For now, however, the legs are small and weak. The tadpole wriggles its body and flicks its tail to push itself forward.

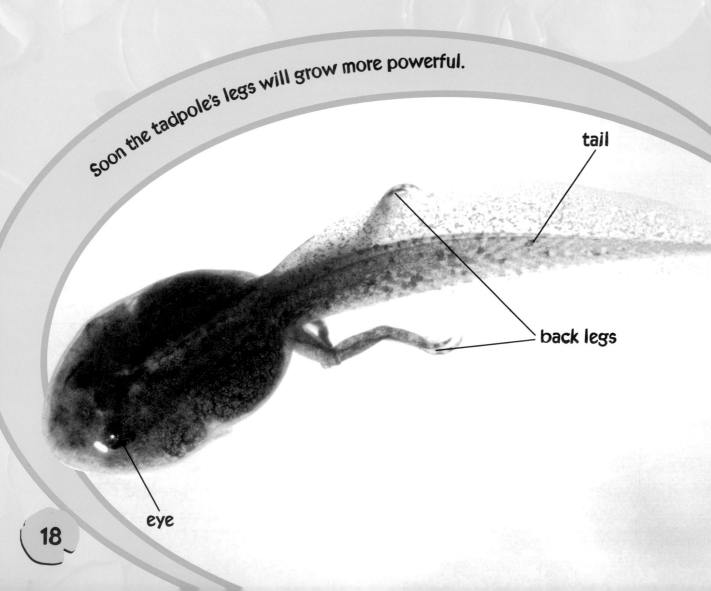

Soon the tadpole's legs will grow more powerful.

tail

back legs

eye

Bottom feeder

The tadpole still spends much of its time near the bottom of the pond. It is safer here, and there is more to eat. The tadpole feeds on the small scraps of plants and dead animals that sink down and settle there.

Escaping danger

The tadpole faces fierce hunters, or **predators**, including fish, newts, diving beetles, water scorpions and dragonfly nymphs. A tadpole cannot swim as quickly as these hunters. Instead, it hides among the lower leaves of pond plants. Its brown body, greenish speckles and see-through tail are good camouflage. This means that the colours help the tadpole to blend in with its surroundings and make it hard to spot.

The dragonfly nymph hunts tadpoles. Its lower jaw can shoot out to grab its **prey**.

Coming up for air

At around six weeks, the tadpole starts to grow **lungs** inside its body. The tadpole can no longer breathe under water like a fish. Instead it breathes air like we do. Lungs remove **oxygen** from air like **gills** remove it from water. The tadpole has to swim up to the surface to take in gulps of air.

These tadpoles are coming up to the surface of the pond to breathe.

Arm buds

The tadpole's back legs are growing bigger and stronger, and its front legs are beginning to form. The six-week-old tadpole already has bulges on its body where its front legs will grow.

Using its strong back legs, the tadpole can power through the water.

front leg is forming

Tadpole cannibal

The tadpole starts eating new foods. As well as plants and some dead insects, the tadpole feasts on other tadpoles – dead ones, that is. Its gut shrinks now that its diet contains more meat and fewer plants. As an adult frog, it will be a carnivore (an animal that eats only meat).

Frog's legs

By ten weeks, the tadpole's front legs have formed. It is a froglet! Like an adult frog, it has four legs. The back legs end in five toes and the front legs end in four toes. The froglet uses all four legs to help it swim.

Other changes make the froglet look more like an adult, too. Its body is changing. Its head starts to take shape. Its mouth becomes wider and its eyes start to bulge out.

The froglet looks more like an adult now, but it still has a tail.

End of the tail

The biggest change of all is that the froglet's tail is getting shorter. By twelve weeks, the tail has almost disappeared. All that is left is a short stump. The rest of the tail has been absorbed, or taken back into the animal's body.

Changing shape

A big body change, like the change from tadpole into frog, has a special name – metamorphosis. Frogs are not the only animals that do this. Other **amphibians** do it too, including newts and salamanders. So do most insects. A caterpillar makes a big body change to turn into its adult form, a butterfly.

This newt tadpole will keep its tail as an adult, but will lose its feathery gills.

Leaps and dives

By fourteen weeks, the froglet looks exactly like an adult, only smaller. It leaves the pond to live on land. Its back legs are soon so powerful the frog can leap more than twelve times its own body length. The frog still visits the pond, because it is a good place to catch insects. As it hunts, it watches out for **predators**. Herons, owls, bats, foxes, cats and snakes all feed on frogs. If it senses danger, the frog slips into the water, out of harm's way.

It is not only animals that feed on froglets. This one has been caught by a meat-eating plant called a Venus flytrap!

Goggle eyes

The frog moves faster through water than on land, thanks to the smooth shape of its body and webbed back feet. Its eyes even have an extra pair of eyelids, which are see-through and act like underwater goggles.

Frogs at risk

Frogs face other dangers besides animal predators. The main threat from humans is pollution. This happens when poisons from farms and factories get into ponds and streams. Frogs are very sensitive to pollution. Poisons can soak into the body through their slimy skin.

The young frog dives into the water to escape danger.

A frog feeds

When the frog first comes out of the pond, it is not much bigger than your fingernail. For the rest of the summer, the frog must eat lots of food. It needs to grow bigger so that it will be able to survive the winter.

A mouthful of fly makes a perfect frog feast.

Sticky tongues

The frog eats small, flying insects. When the frog notices a movement, it flashes out its long, sticky tongue. The insect sticks to the tongue – which snaps back into the frog's mouth like an elastic band.

Eye spy

The frog relies mainly on sight when it is hunting. With its huge, bulging eyes, the frog is able to spot movement in just about any direction.

The frog usually swallows its catch whole. It has small, sharp teeth in the roof of its mouth, but uses these for grabbing hold of **prey**, rather than for chewing. As well as flies, the frog feasts on snails (shell and all!), slugs, worms and crunchy beetles. Delicious!

Gotcha! A frog leaps forward with its sticky tongue to catch insects.

A winter sleep

The frog must find somewhere to spend the winter. Out in the cold it would die, so the frog finds a frost-free place such as a cosy, damp pile of leaves. Another good place is the mud at the bottom of a pond, because the frog can take in enough **oxygen** from the water through its skin to survive. The frog's body slows right down and the frog enters a kind of sleep.

This young frog will stay in the damp soil until spring.

New life

When spring comes, the frog becomes active again. A few types of frog are ready to find a **mate**, but most need to grow for another two or three years. They can then mate and produce their own tadpoles so that the **life cycle** can begin all over again.

Cold-blooded creature

Humans make their own body heat. However hot or cold you feel, your body is usually at a steady 37° Celsius. A frog cannot do this. How hot or cold its body is depends on its surroundings. In freezing weather, the frog will die unless it finds shelter.

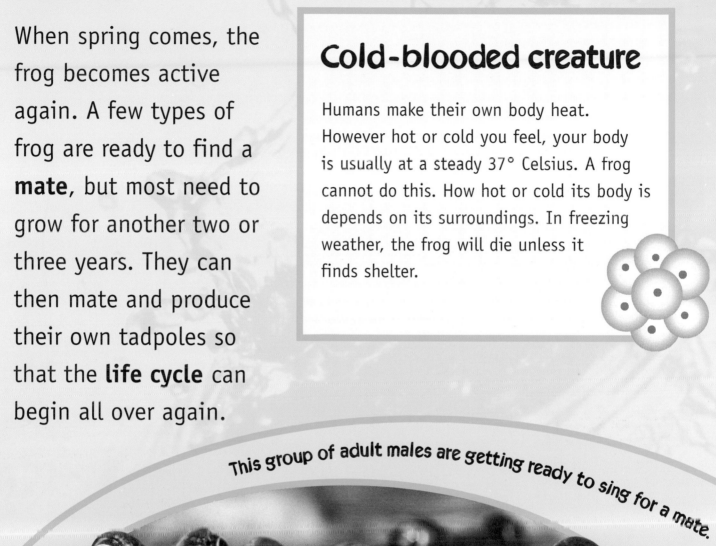

This group of adult males are getting ready to sing for a mate.

Find out for yourself

The best way to find out more about the **life cycle** of a frog is to watch it happen with your own eyes. Perhaps your teacher will let you watch tadpoles develop in a tank in the classroom. You can also find out more by reading books about frogs and other **amphibians**, and by looking for information on the Internet.

Books to read

How Things Grow: From Tadpole to Frog, Sally Morgan (Belitha Press, 2002)
Lifecycles: Frog, Louise Spilsbury (Raintree, 2003)
The Life Cycle of a Frog, Kathryn Smithyman and Bobbie Kalman (Crabtree Publishing Company, 2001)

Using the Internet

Explore the Internet to find out more about frogs. Websites can change, and if some of the links below no longer work, don't worry. Use a search engine, such as www.yahooligans.com, and type in keywords such as 'frog', 'life cycle', 'pond' and 'tadpole'.

Websites

http://allaboutfrogs.org
Find some great pictures of the life cycle of the frog. Plus pages of amazing facts, frog fables and a frog colouring book.
http://www.exploratorium.edu/frogs
An online museum exhibit with facts, pictures, sounds and stories.

Disclaimer
All the Internet addresses (URLs) given in this book were valid at the time of going to press. However, due to the dynamic nature of the Internet, some addresses may have changed, or sites may have ceased to exist since publication. While the author and publishers regret any inconvenience this may cause readers, no responsibility for any such changes can be accepted by either the author or the publishers.

Glossary

abdomen lower part of an animal's body, where it digests food and where its reproductive organs are

adapt slowly change to deal with new conditions

amphibian cold-blooded animal that has a bony skeleton and slimy skin. Frogs, toads and newts are all types of amphibian.

digest break down food inside the body

fertilize join together male and female parts to create the beginnings of a new living thing

frogspawn clump of frog's eggs, each safe in a jelly-like coating

gills feathery body parts that allow underwater animals, such as fish and tadpoles, to take oxygen from water

habitat place where an animal lives

hatch when a young animal comes out of its egg

herbivore animal that only eats plants

life cycle all the different stages in the life of a living thing, such as an animal or plant

lungs balloon-like body parts that allow land animals, such as frogs or humans, to take oxygen from air

mate (noun) animal that can come together with another animal to make eggs or babies

mate (verb) when a male and female animal come together to make eggs or babies

nutrients goodness that feeds an animal or plant

oxygen gas found in air and water. All animals, including humans, need to breathe oxygen in order to stay alive.

predator animal that hunts other animals and eats them for food

prey animal that is hunted by other animals for food

sperm male sex cells

yolk part of an egg that contains food for the growing life inside it

Index